COLLEGE GOATs

THE GREATEST OF ALL TIME

GOATs OF COLLEGE WOMEN'S GYMNASTICS

BY BLYTHE LAWRENCE

SportsZone

An Imprint of Abdo Publishing

abdobooks.com

abdobooks.com

Published by Abdo Publishing, a division of ABDO, PO Box 398166, Minneapolis, Minnesota 55439.

Printed in the United States of America, North Mankato, Minnesota.
102025
012026

Cover Photo: Matthew Hinton/AP Images
Interior Photos: David Madison/Getty Images Sport/Getty Images, 5; Courtesy of Hargrett Rare Book and Manuscript Library/University of Georgia Libraries, 6, 10, 12–13; University of Kentucky/Catapult Sports, 9; Brett Wilhelm/NCAA Photos/Getty Images, 14, 16–17; Cory McKnight/NCAA Photos/Getty Images, 18; Scott Bruhn/NCAA Photos/Getty Images, 20–21; Cliff Williams/NCAA Photos/Getty Images, 22; Nati Harnik/AP Images, 24–25; Michael Wade/Icon SMI/Corbis/Icon Sportswire/Getty Images, 26–27; Katharine Lotze/Getty Images Sport/Getty Images, 29; Kyusung Gong/Icon Sportswire/Getty Images, 30; Keith Gillett/Icon Sportswire/Getty Images, 32–33; C. Morgan Engel/NCAA Photos/Getty Images, 34–35, 40–41; Kyle Okita/Cal Sport Media/ZUMA Wire/AP Images, 36–37; Timothy Nwachukwu/NCAA Photos/Getty Images, 38; Bella Kanelopoulos/LSU/University Images/Getty Images, 42

Editor: Dalton Rains
Series Designer: Kate Liestman

Library of Congress Control Number: 2025939136

Publisher's Cataloging-in-Publication Data

Names: Lawrence, Blythe, author.
Title: GOATs of college women's gymnastics / by Blythe Lawrence
Description: Minneapolis, Minnesota: Abdo Publishing, 2026 | Series: College GOATs: the greatest of all time | Includes online resources and index.
Identifiers: ISBN 9781098298364 (lib. bdg.) | ISBN 9798384932161 (ebook)
Subjects: LCSH: College sports--Juvenile literature. | Gymnastics--Juvenile literature. | Sports records--Juvenile literature. | College sports--Records--Juvenile literature. | Women college athletes--Juvenile literature.
Classification: DDC 796.44--dc23

TABLE OF CONTENTS

KELLY GARRISON

A top American gymnast, Kelly Garrison competed all over the world in the early 1980s. Any college team would have loved to have her. But Garrison stayed close to home. She arrived at the University of Oklahoma in 1985.

Garrison's routines stood out for their difficulty and creativity. Her best apparatus was balance beam. Garrison's full-twisting backward somersault mount earned praise. So did her unique choreography.

In gymnastics, specific moves or positions are known as skills. Garrison sometimes completed moves that had never been done before. When that happens, the skill is named after the gymnast who first performed it. Four skills on beam were named after Garrison. In 1987, the groundbreaking gymnast became the National Collegiate Athletic Association (NCAA) individual all-around champion.

The world's best gymnasts compete in the elite category. College competition is considered one step lower. Other gymnasts chose to focus on either elite or NCAA gymnastics. Almost nobody thought it was possible to do both at the same time. Garrison was up for the challenge. Her college success continued in 1988. In April, she became the first NCAA gymnast to score a perfect 10. Weeks later,

FAST FACT

Over the years, more and more college gymnasts began competing with the US Women's National Team. But for decades, Garrison was the only gymnast to win the NCAA title and compete at the Olympic Games in the same year.

the Sooners star won her second NCAA all-around title. Meanwhile, Garrison was also preparing for elite competition. She placed second at the 1988 US Gymnastics Championships and qualified for the Olympic Trials. There she earned a spot on the US Olympic team. At the 1988 Olympic Games in Seoul, South Korea, Garrison led the team to a fourth-place finish in the all-around.

Kelly Garrison was the captain of the 1988 US Olympic team.

In 1987, Corrinne Wright earned All-America honors for floor exercise and the all-around.

CORRINNE WRIGHT

As the first Black NCAA gymnast at Georgia, Corrinne Wright was a trailblazer. Growing up in New York, she took classes at a local gym. At first, she practiced only a few hours a week. Then she moved to a gym in nearby Connecticut. The new gym was completely focused on gymnastics. Suddenly, she was training 20 hours a week.

Wright thrived in her new environment. By 1985, she was on the US Women's National Team. Next up was college. Oddly, no schools seemed eager to recruit the top athlete. Later, Wright learned why. She was listed as being a year younger than she really was. So NCAA coaches didn't know she was old enough for college.

Despite the confusion, Georgia coach Suzanne Yoculan invited Wright to come for a visit. The tour convinced the gymnast to move down to Georgia. Like she always had, Wright threw herself into training. Soon, her efforts paid off. During her freshman year, Wright lifted Georgia to its first NCAA team championship. In 1989, Georgia won again. Wright also became the first Black gymnast to win the NCAA all-around title.

After graduating, Wright became a coach herself. In 2022, Fisk University in Tennessee decided to start a gymnastics team. It was the first Historically Black College or University to do that. The school wanted a coach who understood the historical importance of the job. Wright was the perfect fit. When talking to recruits, Wright often began with a simple question. She asked, "Do you want to make history?"

JENNY HANSEN

As of 2025, Kentucky's storied men's basketball team had won eight NCAA championships. Kentucky gymnast Jenny Hansen has eight titles too. The difference is that Hansen won hers individually.

Between 1993 and 1995, Hansen was the country's best college gymnast. The Kentucky star racked up 28 perfect scores over the course of her stellar career. During that time, she was the NCAA all-around champion three years in a row. She also won individual titles on vault, balance beam, and floor exercise.

Those kinds of statistics were unheard of before Hansen arrived on the scene. In the 30 years after, only two other gymnasts managed to get as many perfect scores. And only one other athlete won three all-around titles.

Before the 2012 Olympics in London, England, Hansen worked on a TV show about gymnastics. A famous coach also worked on the show. Hansen's skills impressed him. The coach encouraged her to return to competitive gymnastics. So at 38 years old, Hansen made a comeback. She was 20 years older than most of the competition. But Hansen proved that older gymnasts could compete in the elite ranks.

FAST FACT

Until 2006, a 10 was the best possible score in elite gymnastics. Then the scoring system changed in elite gymnastics. But flawless routines are still awarded with perfect 10s at the college level.

Jenny Hansen won nine conference championships with Kentucky.

Karin Lichey won the 1999 Honda Award. This award is given to the NCAA's top gymnast.

KARIN LICHEY

It was February 23, 1996. Georgia freshman Karin Lichey had been on campus for only a few months when the Georgia GymDogs lined up for a meet against the Kentucky Wildcats. Now she was on the cusp of doing something that had never been done.

The opportunity almost didn't happen. Lichey had felt sick before the meet began. She wasn't sure if she would be able to compete. A coach suggested taking the meet one event at a time. Lichey agreed. Her first routine was on vault. She performed a beautiful front handspring front pike half. It earned a perfect 10. The performance set the tone for her night.

In her next event, Lichey scored a 10 on bars. Then she earned another perfect score on beam. By the time she had finished her floor routine, the crowd in Stegeman Coliseum was on its feet. When a final 10 was flashed, the crowd exploded. Coach Suzanne Yoculan jumped for joy. Meanwhile, Lichey took a victory lap around the red floor mat. She was the first NCAA gymnast to score a "perfect 40." That's the total when every routine earns a 10.

Scoring a perfect 40 as a freshman was an extraordinary feat. And Lichey continued performing gorgeous gymnastics for Georgia over the rest of her college career. In both 1998 and 1999, the GymDogs went undefeated and won the NCAA team championship. The run sparked a long reign of success for Georgia.

KIM ARNOLD

Kim Arnold was not a typical Georgia recruit. She grew up in Portland, Oregon. Oregon was across the country from GymDog territory. But Georgia's coaches saw something special in Arnold. They convinced her to make the long journey east.

During her freshman year, Arnold had trouble finding her footing. The team struggled too. Georgia was locked in a pattern. It would perform like one of the best teams in the country. But the team would falter when a big victory was within reach. That was the case in 1997. Three falls off the beam cost the team its chance for the championship.

Still, the instincts of Georgia's coaches turned out to be right. Arnold bounced back to find success. Although Georgia fell short of an NCAA team championship in 1997, Arnold claimed the individual all-around title. Her performance seemed to inspire everyone else.

In 1998, the GymDogs went undefeated during the regular season. They marched into the NCAA Championships with heads held high. Arnold led the way. She won her second consecutive all-around title. But this time the team joined her on top. For the first time since 1993, Georgia finished the season with an NCAA team championship. That year Arnold also scored her first perfect 10 on beam. It was only the third perfect mark on beam by any Georgia gymnast.

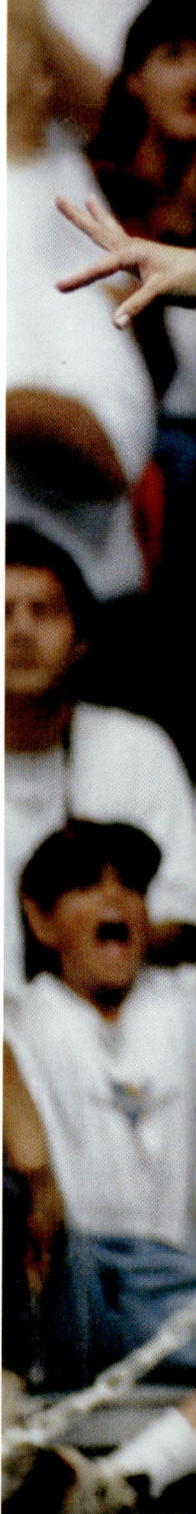

FAST FACT

Kim Arnold wasn't the only gymnast in the family. Her daughter Elena eventually competed in college gymnastics too. Elena joined the Louisiana State University (LSU) Tigers in 2021.

Kim Arnold finished her college career with 21 perfect 10s.

Andreé Pickens was the captain of Alabama's gymnastics team in 2002.

ANDREÉ PICKENS

Andreé Pickens was at the top of her game when an injury threatened to derail her final season. Pickens had been a natural fit for the ambitious Alabama team. Before college, she had competed at the 1996 US Olympic Trials. In her debut NCAA season, she showed she could contend with the best athletes in the country. With her smooth and powerful technique, Pickens excelled on vault and floor. The freshman tied for the 1999 NCAA individual title on beam.

Disaster struck at the end of Pickens's junior year. During a practice, she felt something give out in her leg. Pickens had torn her Achilles tendon. That tendon connects the calf muscle to the heel.

The Achilles tear kept Pickens out of the 2001 NCAA Championships. The injured star watched from the stands as Alabama finished in a disappointing fourth. But Pickens vowed that 2002 would be different. Recovering from the injury was hard and frustrating. She had to take things slowly. But she gradually regained her form.

By the next year, Pickens was fully healed and strong as ever. In 2002, she led Alabama to its first NCAA team championship in six years. She also claimed the NCAA title on bars. Plus, she placed second in all-around and third on vault.

FAST FACT

Pickens also competed as a pole vaulter on Alabama's track-and-field team. She quickly set a new school record. After school, she even made it to the 2008 US Olympic Trials.

ASHLEY MILES

After years as an individual competitor, Ashley Miles longed to be part of a team. Meanwhile, Alabama needed a new leader to replace departed star Andreé Pickens. It was a win-win for Miles and the Crimson Tide.

Thanks to several years on the US Women's National Team, Miles already had great technique. She also flourished in the spotlight. Alabama coach Sarah Patterson said Miles was like a basketball player who "wants the ball in her hands on the last shot."

At 5-foot-7, Miles was usually the tallest gymnast at any NCAA meet. She was so tall that Patterson put her in the anchor position in the team lineup. That was very unusual for a freshman gymnast. The anchor performs last for the team. Patterson reasoned that Miles was so tall and strong that anyone who went after her would seem less impressive. Miles's height advantage was most obvious on vault. She could travel long distances in the air. Everything about her gymnastics was big.

Between 2003 and 2006, nobody was able to touch Alabama's new star. Miles won three NCAA vault titles. She was also the national champion on floor exercise in 2004. Along the way, she piled up a total of 11 perfect 10s. That set an Alabama record. She was also the second gymnast to record two perfect scores in the team final at the NCAA Championships. Altogether, her accomplishments made her a giant among Alabama's champions.

Ashley Miles performs a title-winning floor routine at the 2004 NCAA Championships.

FAST FACT

During her senior year, Mohini Bhardwaj scored a near-perfect 39.975 in the all-around event. That was the second-highest total ever recorded.

In 2000, Mohini Bhardwaj won the NCAA individual title on bars.

MOHINI BHARDWAJ

Life as a University of California, Los Angeles (UCLA), gymnast was very different from what Mohini Bhardwaj had experienced as a teenager. Bhardwaj grew up with the Olympics on her mind. She dreamed of competing with the best in the world.

When Bhardwaj was 16, her coach moved to Texas. The young gymnast followed. Even though she was still a teenager, Bhardwaj lived in her own apartment. She grew up fast. By the time she enrolled at UCLA, Bhardwaj had been living alone for several years. College gymnastics started to bring much-needed discipline to Bhardwaj's life.

In 1997, the year before Bhardwaj arrived, UCLA had captured its first NCAA team championship. The Bruins were the first team to break the hold Utah, Georgia, and Alabama had on the top prize. Those three schools had won all 15 NCAA titles to date.

Georgia rebounded to win NCAA titles in Bhardwaj's first two seasons with UCLA. But the Bruins proved their success wasn't a fluke during her junior and senior seasons. Bhardwaj led UCLA to two straight titles in 2000 and 2001.

After college, Bhardwaj felt she still had the skills of an Olympian. At 25, she was considered extremely old for a female gymnast. Bhardwaj proved the naysayers wrong by making the US Women's National Team. She delivered a key performance on beam to help the United States win silver at the 2004 Olympic Games in Athens, Greece. Partly because of that performance, people think differently about age in gymnastics today.

JAMIE DANTZSCHER

Few NCAA gymnasts can boast of receiving a perfect 10 during their four years of college. Jamie Dantzscher earned one with the first routine she performed as a UCLA Bruin.

From the very beginning of her time at UCLA, Dantzscher played an important role in breaking the dominance of Utah, Georgia, and Alabama. In her 2001 debut, she picked up perfect scores on uneven bars and floor exercise. Her results stunned the NCAA gymnastics world.

But that performance was only the start. During her four years at UCLA, Dantzscher led the Bruins to three NCAA team championships. She also won individual titles in the all-around, as well as on vault, bars, and floor. The experience was marvelous for Bruins fans. It was also encouraging for Dantzscher. She had struggled with many parts of elite gymnastics.

In all, the UCLA star scored 28 perfect 10s. That tied Jenny Hansen's record. In a 2004 meet, Dantzscher led UCLA to a towering score of 198.875. That tied an NCAA record. Dantzscher contributed a 10 on bars to the effort.

Dantzscher's impact on the sport continued after she was done competing. In 2016, she spoke out about being sexually abused by a former US team doctor. This brave step helped uncover wider abuse within the sport.

In 2002, Jamie Dantzscher scored seven perfect 10s in a row on floor exercise.

Tasha Schwikert finished her college career with a total of four perfect 10s.

TASHA SCHWIKERT

By the time she arrived on the UCLA campus at the end of 2004, Tasha Schwikert seemed to have done it all. She had already been to the Olympics. In fact, Schwikert was the youngest member of the US Women's National Team at the 2000 Games in Sydney, Australia. Three years later, she was the captain of the first US team to win the gold medal at the World Championships. College gymnastics was the final frontier.

Schwikert was a mature gymnast by the time she came to UCLA. She had postponed her college career while trying to make the 2004 Olympic team. That meant she was already 20 by the time she enrolled. While technically a freshman, Schwikert came into college with the experience of a junior.

A balanced gymnast, Schwikert excelled on every apparatus. She also stepped into the team leader role, taking over where Jamie Dantzscher had left off. Schwikert made an instant impact on the team. As a freshman, she won the 2005 all-around title. She won it again in 2008. That made her UCLA's first two-time individual champion.

Winning all-around titles three years apart was something unique. No other two-time NCAA champion had managed it. Schwikert left UCLA with three NCAA titles. She added an uneven bars title to the two in all-around. Schwikert is remembered as one of the best ever to wear the Bruins' blue and gold. The Pacific-12 Conference honored her in 2016 by naming Schwikert its Gymnast of the Century.

COURTNEY KUPETS

Big things were expected of Courtney Kupets when she committed to compete for Georgia in the early 2000s. Kupets was one of Georgia's most accomplished recruits ever. At 18 years old, she was already a world champion and an Olympic medalist on bars.

Despite the high expectations, Kupets exceeded coaches' and fans' wildest hopes. In her four years of college, Kupets rewrote Georgia's record books. Her athletic style and crisp landings left little for judges to criticize. But what really set Kupets apart was her consistency. The gymnast almost never made a mistake.

However, Kupets always strove to do better. That helped her capture three NCAA all-around titles between 2006 and 2009, tying Jenny Hansen's accomplishment from more than a decade earlier. The Georgia star also overcame a serious Achilles tendon injury in her junior year. That injury kept her from competing at the 2008 NCAA Championships. However, she returned in 2009 as dominant as ever. In her final competition, Kupets took the NCAA titles for all-around, bars, and beam. She also tied for the title on floor exercise.

FAST FACT

Courtney Kupets won a total of nine individual NCAA titles. That made her the most decorated gymnast in NCAA history.

Courtney Kupets won four NCAA team championships with Georgia.

Bridget Sloan finished college with six individual titles.

BRIDGET SLOAN

The Florida Gators had come close to winning an NCAA team championship. But for all their talent, they always fell just short of winning it all. The Gators finished fifth in 2010 and were runners-up two years later.

Bridget Sloan's arrival in 2013 made the difference. The Indiana native arrived with a huge list of accomplishments already. In 2008, she had helped the United States win an Olympic team silver medal. Then she won US and world all-around titles in 2009. Sloan became the first world all-around champion to compete in the NCAA. And the accomplished gymnast brought her winning mindset to Florida.

Like UCLA's Tasha Schwikert, Sloan was already 20 as a freshman. Years of experience had taught her how to win. And she backed it up with hard work in the gym. It all came together when she stepped up to compete.

At her first NCAA Championships in 2013, Sloan led the Gators to a team title at last. She also claimed the all-around title and another gold on the balance beam. But Sloan was just getting started.

During the next two years, Sloan's performances helped Florida capture two more NCAA team championships. The Gators tied with Oklahoma in 2014 before winning outright in 2015. The school couldn't quite snag a fourth-consecutive title in 2016, but Sloan remained the gymnast to beat in the NCAA. At the 2016 NCAA Championships, Sloan was once again the all-around champion. She closed out her college career with the individual titles on bars and beam as well.

KYLA ROSS

When she stepped up to the uneven bars in UCLA's first meet of the 2017 season, Kyla Ross was making history. The Bruins were lucky to have landed Ross after she was heavily recruited by many different schools. At just 15 years old, she had been a member of "The Fierce Five" US Olympic team. She helped the United States take home a gold medal in 2012.

Ross decided to stay in elite gymnastics after the 2012 Games. She felt she had more to accomplish. Five years and numerous accolades later, she was finally ready to make her UCLA debut. Ross and her new teammate Madison Kocian became the first Olympic gold medalists to compete in NCAA gymnastics.

Ross quickly impressed fans with her calm, smooth style. The focused and driven gymnast was just as successful in the NCAA as she had been at the elite level. By her senior year, she'd earned the nickname "Kyla Boss."

Because of the COVID-19 pandemic, the 2020 NCAA season ended early. Ross didn't get to compete in the NCAA Championships in her final year. But she had piled up many wins in the three previous years. Between 2017 and 2019, Ross won or tied for a share of the titles on every individual apparatus. She retired as the first gymnast to win titles at the Olympics, the World Championships, and the NCAA Championships.

In 2019, Kyla Ross recorded a perfect score in 10 straight meets.

Katelyn Ohashi performs her floor routine at a 2019 meet.

KATELYN OHASHI

Competing for UCLA restored Katelyn Ohashi's love of gymnastics. Her delight was evident as she stepped up to perform her new floor routine on January 12, 2019. For 90 seconds, Ohashi poured her heart and soul into the exercise set to a medley of classic rock and pop songs. The performance felt like more than a routine. It seemed to be an expression of Ohashi's personality, with the 21-year-old expressing herself through dance.

Video footage of Ohashi's routine went viral. Ohashi's joy while performing pulled people in. And the effect wasn't felt just online. UCLA traveled to Ohashi's hometown of Seattle, Washington, for a dual meet with the University of Washington a few weeks later. Ohashi was so popular that Washington set a record for ticket sales.

Before long, Ohashi was an international sensation. She appeared in commercials and traveled the world performing. By 2025, her video had been viewed more than 240 million times.

Ohashi's success didn't come without hardships. As a young teenager, she had been touted as an Olympic prospect. Ohashi won the prestigious American Cup in 2013. But numerous injuries took their toll. She quit elite gymnastics afterward.

Six years later, Ohashi had the nation's attention. She seized the opportunity to speak frankly about her early struggles in the sport. "I've said before, 'gymnastics is abusive,' but now I know it's not the sport that's abusive," she said. "It's the culture that was created and accepted and normalized."

MAGGIE NICHOLS

Maggie Nichols brought many talents to Oklahoma. One was the ability to make things look effortless. This certainly applied to Nichols's gymnastics. But it also applied to her life, which was anything but easy before she joined the NCAA.

As a 10-year-old, Nichols attended a summer gymnastics camp in Norman, Oklahoma, and connected with coach K. J. Kindler. She decided then that Oklahoma would be her school. But before that, she wanted to go to the Olympics.

Nichols showed that she was Olympic material at the 2015 World Championships. She helped the US Women's National Team win a gold medal and also earned a bronze medal for her floor routine. But behind the scenes, something dark was happening. Nichols was being abused by US team doctor Larry Nassar.

In 2015, Nichols's coach overheard her talking to another gymnast about what Nassar had done. The coach reported the conversation. It was the beginning of Nassar's downfall. Nichols became "Athlete A." She was the first athlete to speak out about what was happening. But because of an injury, she was not selected for the Olympic team.

Nichols bore the disappointment with grace. Her years at Oklahoma were a healing period. It showed when she competed. She captured the NCAA all-around title in 2018 and 2019. She also tied for titles on vault, bars, and floor. Plus, Oklahoma won the team championship in 2017 and 2019. Though her final season was cut short by the COVID-19 pandemic, Nichols was already a Sooner legend.

Maggie Nichols piled up a total of eight perfect scores in 2018.

FAST FACT

A gym slam is when a gymnast gets a perfect 10 on every apparatus at least once in her career. Only 14 women have recorded gym slams. Most of them have done it only once. Trinity Thomas achieved it a record five times!

Trinity Thomas's floor routine scored a perfect 10 at the 2022 NCAA Championships.

TRINITY THOMAS

Trinity Thomas was a natural athlete. In high school, she made a name for herself as a potential star in gymnastics. But the young athlete didn't just compete as a gymnast. She competed in diving too.

Participating in multiple sports was unusual for an elite gymnast. The top athletes generally focused on just one. Thomas was different. She refused to limit herself.

As a result, the multi-skilled athlete arrived at the University of Florida fresh and full of energy. In her freshman year, Thomas competed all-around in every meet. She proved very difficult to beat. In fact, Thomas racked up 26 event titles in her first season. As a sophomore, she added another 28 wins. By the end of her college career, Thomas had a school record of 113 event titles.

In the 2022 NCAA Championships, Thomas won titles for all-around, bars, and floor exercise. Then, Thomas gained an extra year of NCAA eligibility due to the COVID-19 pandemic. She remained a force. In her final NCAA Championships in 2023, Thomas earned a 10 on vault, closing out her career with a perfect score. It also marked the 28th perfect 10 of Thomas's career, tying the record held by Jenny Hansen and Jamie Dantzscher.

NATALIE WOJCIK

In 2021, Natalie Wojcik was part of a Cinderella story. In her case, the ball took place at the NCAA Championships. But Wojcik and her Michigan Wolverines teammates were not expected to be the center of attention.

The Wolverines had been fairly successful. They often took first place at the Big Ten Conference Championships. But the team was not considered a contender for the national title. UCLA, Florida, LSU, and Oklahoma were the hottest teams in the NCAA. Up until 2021, Michigan's best season had ended with a third-place finish. Wojcik had been two years old at the time.

Like her team, Wojcik was a good gymnast who couldn't quite make it to the very top. By 2021, she was a junior and having her best performances yet. However, the first part of the 2021 postseason didn't go Michigan's way. The Wolverines finished second at the conference championships. The team improved with a solid performance in the semifinals of the NCAA Championships.

Michigan's story might have ended there. Then everything changed. The Wolverines had a dream performance. They surprised everyone with a title-winning 198.250 points. That was the third-best team score ever recorded at the championships.

Wojcik was at the center of it all. The elegant Michigan star delivered two of the team's highest scores on beam and floor. Wojcik's sleek performances came as near to perfection as any gymnast's that night. Michigan finally had a title. With her teammates, Wojcik had taken part in an unforgettable piece of NCAA gymnastics history.

Natalie Wojcik scored a 9.9875 on beam at the 2021 NCAA Championships.

LYNNZEE BROWN

Lynnzee Brown never thought she was NCAA material. Throughout high school, the Missouri native doubted whether she was good enough to compete in college. While her gym produced Olympians, Brown didn't think she matched up with the country's best gymnasts.

During her college career, Lynnzee Brown recorded two perfect scores on bars.

However, Denver University's coaches were interested. They kept calling the gym. Finally, one of her coaches suggested she look into the opportunity. She hesitantly agreed.

Brown became the first member of her family to go to a four-year college. She had to get used to many new things. But she was pleasantly surprised to find out that she was competitive in the NCAA. Brown's team embraced her. Little by little, she began to feel at home.

Positive results came quickly. Soon, Brown was ranked among the best gymnasts in the country. In 2019, she tied for the NCAA floor title with three other gymnasts, including Olympic champion Kyla Ross. There was no question about it: Brown belonged.

Brown's coaches urged her to compete on an even bigger stage. So she applied to represent Haiti, her father's country. In 2023, she became the first Haitian gymnast to compete at the World Championships. A year later, she competed at the Olympic Games in Paris, France. She became Haiti's first gymnast to compete at the Olympics. All this from a gymnast who went to college wondering whether she belonged.

FAST FACT

Four Denver University gymnasts have competed at the Olympics. Jessica Lopez represented Venezuela at the Games in 2008, 2012, and 2016. Simona Castro of Chile qualified in 2012 and 2016. And Annamari Maaranen competed for Finland in 2008.

JADE CAREY

Just weeks after winning gold on floor at the Tokyo, Japan, Olympics in 2021, Jade Carey finally enrolled at Oregon State. The Beavers had waited a long time for the outstanding recruit. Carey had postponed college for three years while she tried to make the US Olympic Team. She soon showed that she was worth the wait.

At the elite level, Carey's calling card was high-energy tumbling. Many elite gymnasts ease up on difficulty when they go to college. Carey didn't see the need. Her opening tumbling pass on floor was a double-twisting double tuck. Few NCAA gymnasts would even dream of doing that skill. For Carey, it was routine.

Carey quickly established herself as one of the most dependable gymnasts in the country. Heading into her senior season with the Beavers in 2025, she had 117 individual event titles. That was a school record.

Carey balanced NCAA competition with her international career. Other athletes have mostly done one at a time. Carey managed both at the same time.

Competing for the US Women's National Team in the college offseason, Carey won two gold medals and a bronze at the 2022 World Championships. At the 2024 Olympics, she helped the United States earn team gold. She also took bronze on vault. Five months later, she was back competing for Oregon State. The senior earned four perfect 10s that season. That brought her career total to 16. Carey left behind a legacy as one of the Beavers' best ever.

In the 2024 NCAA Championships, Jade Carey placed second in the all-around and on floor.

Haleigh Bryant was named the Southeastern Conference Gymnast of the Year in 2024.

HALEIGH BRYANT

The LSU Tigers were always among the top teams in the nation. But the team was missing one thing before Haleigh Bryant came along. LSU had never won an NCAA team championship.

Before 2024, the Tigers had been Southeastern Conference champions. A few of their gymnasts had won individual NCAA titles too. Bryant was determined to lead LSU to its first team title. She was one of the most aerodynamic vaulters and tumblers ever to compete for LSU. Bryant strove for greatness in each of her years with the Tigers.

During her first season, Bryant became the most decorated freshman in program history. She won the NCAA title on vault. The 2024 season went even better. In February, Bryant completed a gym slam with her first perfect 10 on beam. In March, she set a school record in the all-around with a score of 39.925.

The Tigers went undefeated in 23 straight meets before the NCAA Championships. Then, in April, they finally brought home a team title. LSU defeated California, Utah, and Florida to stand alone as the best in the nation.

Bryant was one of the team's keys to victory. In addition to the team title, she earned the NCAA individual all-around title. It was the last of 30 all-around victories by Bryant during her four years of college. That added yet another school record to her résumé.

HONORABLE MENTIONS

MEGAN McCUNNIFF

In the early 1980s, McCunniff became the first gymnast to win back-to-back NCAA all-around titles. She remained dedicated to Utah's success after graduating. She was a longtime assistant coach and later co-head coach of the Red Rocks.

MISSY MARLOWE

Marlowe won or tied for five NCAA titles during her golden year in 1992. The Utah star was also the first to score a 10 on every event at least once during her NCAA career.

KRISTIN MALONEY

A 2000 Olympic team bronze medalist with the United States, Maloney overcame major injuries to thrive as part of UCLA's superstrong teams in the early 2000s.

JEANA RICE

The daughter of 1972 US Olympian Joan Moore, Rice was the 2004 NCAA all-around champion and a major part of Alabama's success in the 2000s.

ASHLEY POSTELL

Postell was the strongest Utah gymnast of her era and won an NCAA beam title to go with her World Championships gold medal.

ALEX McMURTRY

The ultra-talented McMurtry was the 2017 NCAA all-around champion and one of the key drivers of Florida's immense success.

SAMANTHA PESZEK

A 2008 Olympic silver medalist with Team USA, Peszek went on to have a successful collegiate career at UCLA. She was among the first US Olympic medalists to do NCAA gymnastics after the Games.

ANASTASIA WEBB

Webb, the 2021 NCAA all-around champion, was a bars and beam standout during Oklahoma's golden period in the late 2010s and early 2020s.

GLOSSARY

accolade
An award or accomplishment.

aerodynamic
The qualities of an object that affect how easily it is able to move through the air.

all-around
A gymnastics competition in which athletes compete in all four apparatuses.

apparatus
A type of equipment used during a gymnastics competition.

choreography
The arrangement of steps and movements for a dance or routine.

legacy
How a person or team is remembered.

mature
Having traits and behaviors associated with adulthood.

medley
A musical piece that combines parts of several different songs.

pandemic
A widespread outbreak of a disease that affects a large portion of the population.

recruit
To try to convince a high school athlete to join a college team. The athletes themselves are also called recruits.

routine
A set performance by a gymnast on one apparatus.

MORE INFORMATION

BOOKS

Loh, Stefanie. *Who Is Simone Biles?* Penguin Workshop, 2023.

McDougall, Chrös. *Everything Gymnastics*. Abdo, 2025.

Rule, Heather. *All about Women's College Gymnastics*. Abdo, 2021.

ONLINE RESOURCES

To learn more about the GOATs of college women's gymnastics, please visit **abdobooklinks.com** or scan this QR code. These links are routinely monitored and updated to provide the most current information available.

INDEX

ABOUT THE AUTHOR

Blythe Lawrence is a sports journalist from Seattle, Washington, who has covered gymnastics at four Olympic Games.